Manatee mom and calf

Starry moray eel

Sea otter

ANIMAL
BITES

ocean
animals

Laaren Brown

Flying mobula ray

how to use this book

Look for these colorful tabs to guide your Animal Bites adventure.

where they live **Explore different animal habitats and ecosystems**

bottlenose dolphin **When you see a tab this color, get a close-up look at amazing animals**

how they live **Learn how animals behave and adapt to their environment**

vista **See awesome photos that show the places animals live**

big data **Find the facts and figures**

animal gallery **Take a look at animal similarities and differences**

living/working **conservation**

Find out different ways people interact with animals and their habitats

Just like me
Look for this feature to see how animals behave and live like humans.

table of contents

In the zone

The deeper in the ocean you go, the less sunlight there is. Some animals always live in one zone, while others travel between zones to hunt and feed.

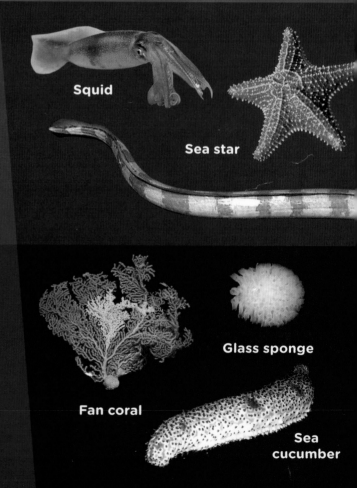

0–600 feet
THE SUNLIGHT ZONE

The sunlight zone teems with life. This is where almost all sea creatures live, including many sharks and smaller fish, mammals, turtles, and sea birds. Plants and plankton live here, too.

Green sea turtle

Pearly razorfish

Bigeye tuna

600-3,300 feet
THE TWILIGHT ZONE

Most of the creatures that live on the seafloor are found in the twilight zone. Only filtered sunlight reaches here, so the light is dim. Many animals in this zone have big eyes or glow in the dark.

Squid

Sea star

3,300-13,000 feet
THE MIDNIGHT ZONE

The midnight zone is pitch black and cold. Animals here have special ways of finding food in the dark. The deepest part of this zone is called the abyss.

Fan coral

Glass sponge

Sea cucumber

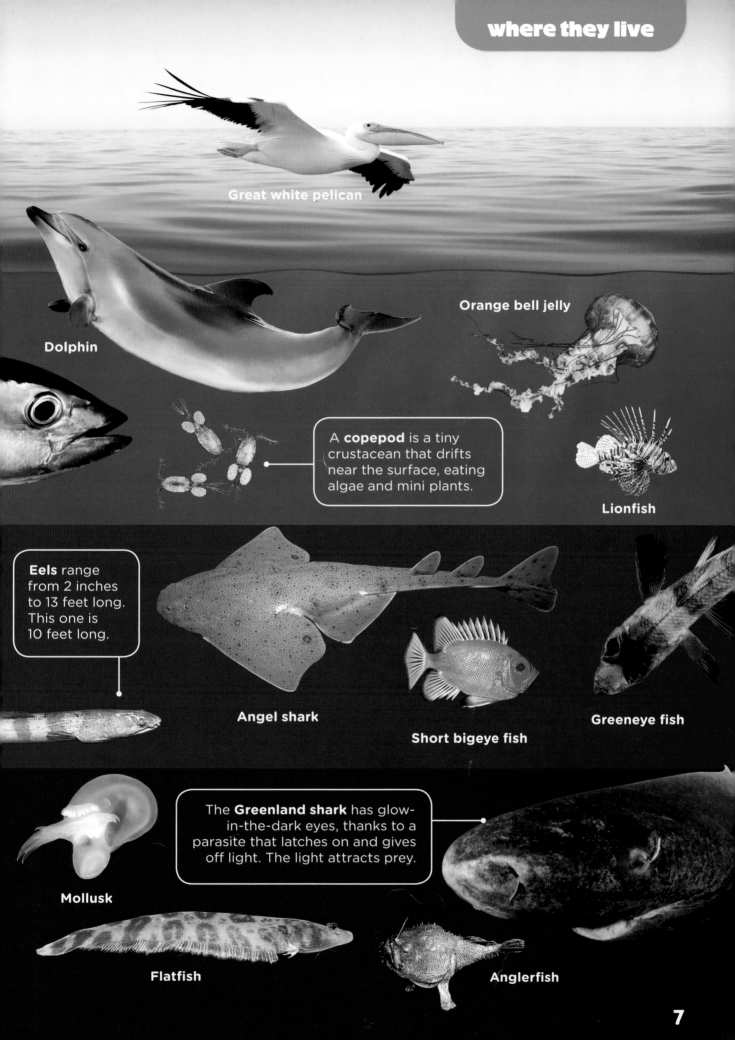

Great white pelican

Dolphin

Orange bell jelly

A **copepod** is a tiny crustacean that drifts near the surface, eating algae and mini plants.

Lionfish

Eels range from 2 inches to 13 feet long. This one is 10 feet long.

Angel shark

Short bigeye fish

Greeneye fish

Mollusk

The **Greenland shark** has glow-in-the-dark eyes, thanks to a parasite that latches on and gives off light. The light attracts prey.

Flatfish

Anglerfish

Life in the deep blue

In some places it's freezing cold. In other places, it's so hot. And it's salty all over. How do ocean animals survive in a world of water?

Clownfish

Like jellies, sea anemones sting. But clownfish don't get stung—a mucus coating on their skin protects them. Their bright colors attract prey that feeds the anemone.

Anglerfish

Angling is another name for fishing. The anglerfish fishes by wiggling a special spine that sticks out of its forehead. When a hungry fish comes along, it thinks the wiggling is a worm and comes to take a look. It gets close . . . closer . . . *chomp*!

Albatross

These huge seabirds can fly almost 10,000 miles in a single flight. To save energy on long journeys, they yo-yo up and down just over the surface of the water.

Arctic cod

The arctic cod lives in some of the coldest water on Earth. But it doesn't freeze. Its blood has a special protein that keeps the cod going, even in water that's nearly ice.

Jellies

Jellies are soft and squishy, but they can still protect themselves and catch prey. The box jelly has more than 5,000 stingers called nematocysts on each long tentacle. Each stinger can blast predators (or dinner) with a powerful zap. The jelly takes in food through a hole in the center of its bell.

It's a family affair

Do you have a big family? Dolphins do! As many as 12 dolphins make up a single family group, called a pod. They play games, they fish, they splash. And just as in many families, pod members sound like they're speaking a language that's all their own.

A dolphin breathes through a **blowhole** on the top of its head.

The **snout**, or **beak**, is the dolphin's mouth. It contains lots of sharp teeth.

Just like me

A dolphin's pectoral fins have bones similar to the ones in your hand, wrist, and arm. They help with swimming and balance.

CLEVER FRIEND?

[X] YES   [ ] NO

Dolphins are smart, sociable creatures. They can communicate with each other and know how to work together.

The **tail** moves up and down as the dolphin swims. This is different from a fish, which moves its tail from side to side.

INFO BITES

Name: Bottlenose Dolphin

Type of animal: Mammal

Home: Every ocean except the Arctic and the Southern

Size: This dolphin is up to 12 feet long and 440 pounds—the size of two dads.

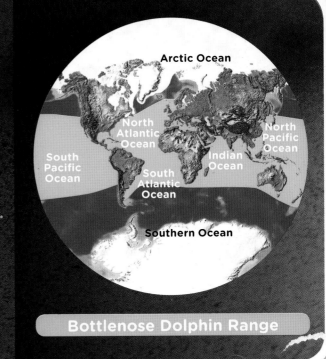

Arctic Ocean

North Atlantic Ocean

North Pacific Ocean

South Pacific Ocean

South Atlantic Ocean

Indian Ocean

Southern Ocean

Bottlenose Dolphin Range

Everybody into the pool!

Animals play in their watery home just like we play in our homes. Sometimes they play for fun, and sometimes their tricks help them in other ways.

Cannonball!

People can't leap out of the water like whales do. But we can have lots of fun jumping into the water!

Hide and seek

Never play hide and seek with an octopus. The octopus will win every time! It can change color and texture to blend in with its surroundings.

Play ball!

When a puffer fish puffs up, it makes a great ball for fun-loving sea lions.

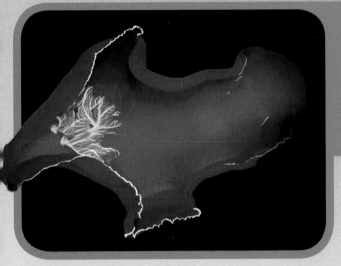

Dance break!

This sea slug whirls through the water, twirling its many-layered mantle. It's called a Spanish dancer because it looks like it's dancing!

Jumping jacks

Huge whales can jump right out of the water! That's called breaching. Some experts think it's a way for whales to communicate—when they smash down on the water, the sound can be heard for long distances.

Amazing rays

Smoothly flapping its wings, the manta ray glides through the ocean.

Fin-tastic

The great white shark is a top ocean predator. It feeds on sea lions, seals, fish, rays, and squid—up to 11 tons of them a year. A shark uses its mouth to find out if something is food. Bites on humans are rare.

Just like me

The great white shark is the only shark that will poke its head out of the water. It's checking out what—or who—is nearby.

AQUARIUM-WORTHY?

☐ YES ☒ NO

Great whites are open-water fish. They can't survive long when kept in captivity.

A **white underside** makes the shark difficult to see from below.

Water passing over the **gills** allows the shark to breathe, A great white must keep moving or it will drown.

Jagged, **triangular teeth** are ready to bite whatever seems like a good meal. The shark has more than 300 teeth.

INFO BITES

Name: Great White Shark

Type of animal: Fish

Home: Warm coastal waters

Size: It grows to an average of 15 feet long, although some great whites can reach 20 feet long. That's the length of a pickup truck.

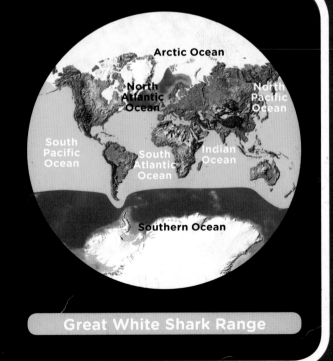

Arctic Ocean

North Atlantic Ocean

North Pacific Ocean

South Pacific Ocean

South Atlantic Ocean

Indian Ocean

Southern Ocean

Great White Shark Range

17

Liquid locomotion

People need to get from one place to another, and most animals do, too. When ocean creatures travel, they move and groove in lots of different ways.

Speed demons

Sailfish have been clocked swimming at almost 70 miles per hour. The fish uses its tail to propel itself forward and up, taking huge leaps out of the water.

Just like me

Jumping as high as a sailfish may be hard without a boost. A trampoline is just the thing to give you extra airtime.

Easy does it

A jelly uses less energy to travel than any other swimming animal. It opens its bell-like top to draw in water. It then squeezes its bell, getting an extra push as the trapped water rushes out.

18

Jet setting

With its long, webbed arms trailing like a black cape, a vampire squid swims by jet propulsion. It sucks water into a special sac in its body, and then squirts water out through a siphon.

R-eel smooth

A long, muscular fish, the moray eel swims through the water in an undulating motion, in the same way as a snake moves. It is one of the few fish that can swim backward.

Hurdles for turtles

Green sea turtles lay eggs on the same beaches where they were born. A female digs a hole in the sand, then lays her eggs and returns to the sea. When the babies hatch, they can take days to dig themselves free—then they crawl to the ocean to begin their lives.

The **built-in shell** is streamlined for smooth swimming.

The **flippers** do not retract into the sea turtle's shell.

INFO BITES

Name: Green Sea Turtle

Type of animal: Reptile

Home: The Atlantic green sea turtle is native to waters around Europe and North America. The eastern Pacific green sea turtle is found from the West Coast of the US to Chile.

Size: Up to 700 pounds and 5 feet long—the length of two tennis rackets.

North America

North Pacific Ocean

Europe

North Atlantic Ocean

Chile

South Pacific Ocean

South America

Green Sea Turtle Range

SEA-PAL-
WORTHY?

[X] YES [ ] No

Sea turtles are gentle animals, and they are fast swimmers. You can swim with them, but you might have a hard time keeping up.

The **skin** is tan colored. The turtle is named for the green color of its muscles.

A **serrated beak** snips sea grasses and scrapes off algae that the turtle eats.

Just like me

A green sea turtle likes the water more than the beach. It will only come on land when it's time for it to nest.

Swimming on a full stomach

Like people, animals in the ocean have their favorite foods, and they've developed many clever ways to put food on the "table."

Handy!

Marlins and other billfish have a built-in fork to pierce their food. We have built-in tools, too—our hands!

Eating right

A right whale gulps large amounts of water, and then filters it through hornlike growths called baleen plates in its mouth. Water passes through the filters back into the ocean, but zooplankton get stuck. A right whale eats about 2,600 pounds of food a day. Birds hover nearby to catch leftovers.

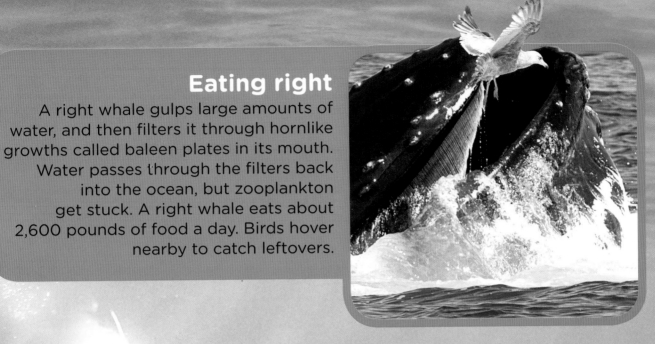

A sea star can push its stomach outside its body and begin digesting food at once. The stomach of this sun sea star is bulging out to devour algae.

Buried treasure

A ray cruises the ocean floor, exposing hidden prey by "wing flapping" to stir up the seabed. Its mouth is on the underside of its body, so the ray can use it to dig around the ocean floor and vacuum up its victims.

Flying high

Albatrosses almost never touch dry land. They can dip down and grab prey in flight. These seabirds sail on wind currents, traveling thousands of miles without landing. Their huge wings hold them up as they glide up and down over the surface of the ocean.

The **hooked beak** is useful for snatching squid and other prey from the water.

Keen eyesight helps the albatross spot prey in the ocean below.

GOOD-LUCK CHARM?

☒ ☒
YES NO

Sailors consider it a sign of good luck when an albatross follows their boat. It's bad luck to harm one.

The **powerful wings** lock into position so the bird can catch the wind.

Just like me

Sometimes an albatross will follow a ship for an easy meal of discarded food. Do you ever eat leftovers?

The **webbed feet** are used for power and steering when swimming.

INFO BITES

Name: Wandering Albatross

Type of animal: Bird

Home: Southern Pacific Ocean

Size: They weigh up to 22 pounds and have a wingspan up to 11 feet wide, making them record-holders for the largest wingspan of all birds. That's as long as two pairs of skis laid end to end.

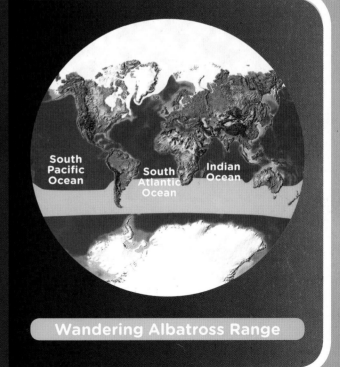

South Pacific Ocean

South Atlantic Ocean

Indian Ocean

Wandering Albatross Range

Letting off steam

On the deepest part of the ocean floor, below the midnight zone, living things huddle around volcanic vents that spew hot, mineral-rich water. The harsh environment is home to many deep-sea creatures.

Deep-sea mussels

Deep-sea mussels thrive around hydrothermal vents. These plentiful mollusks are beneficial to others— bacteria on their shells serve as food for small crabs.

Yeti crab

The yeti crab is hairy, white, and blind—it doesn't have eyes, and doesn't need them. It feels its way around.

Giant tubeworm

The giant tubeworm stays close to hydrothermal vents and eats the bacteria that live nearby. It uses its red plume to absorb oxygen. The worm retracts its plume when threatened.

Pompeii worm

The deep-sea Pompeii worm—
named after a town in Italy that
was destroyed by a volcano—
lives in water that is
bubbling and superhot.

Hydrothermal vents

Hydrothermal vents form around
underground volcanic activity. Cold
water seeps below the seafloor, gets
superheated, and spews upward.

Whale sharks are the biggest fish in the ocean—and they grow so big by eating some of the smallest living things. They gulp large amounts of seawater and filter out tiny plant and animal plankton to eat.

Just like me
Whale sharks sometimes cough to clear their filters, just like you cough to clear your throat.

Speckles help camouflage the shark from above.

The **big mouth** stays open as the shark swims, gathering plankton-filled water.

The **skin** is up to 4 inches thick.

The **powerful tail** can kill a diver who is swimming too close.

INFO BITES

Name: Whale Shark

Type of animal: Fish

Home: Whale sharks like warm water. They are found all over the tropics.

Size: Up to 41 feet long and 47,000 pounds—as big as a school bus.

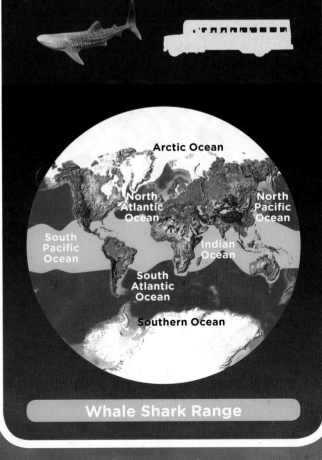

Arctic Ocean

North Atlantic Ocean

North Pacific Ocean

South Pacific Ocean

Indian Ocean

South Atlantic Ocean

Southern Ocean

Whale Shark Range

POOL-PARTY PAL?

☐ YES ☒ NO

Whale sharks are gentle giants that won't eat you, but they're way too big to fit into a swimming pool.

Little, big, biggest

All life in the ocean is connected. Tiny plants are the most plentiful ocean food, and are eaten by bigger creatures. Animals at the top of the food web aren't hunted—they do the hunting.

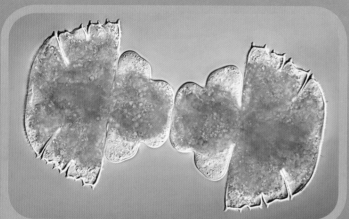

Tons of tidbits

Vast quantities of tiny phytoplankton live near the surface of the ocean. They get energy from the sun. Animal plankton, called zooplankton, feed on these mini plants and are in turn eaten by bigger animals.

Fast times

A dolphin is a top predator. It hunts big prey, including octopus and squid, although it also snacks on little mackerels. It can speed along at more than 20 miles per hour in search of a tasty treat.

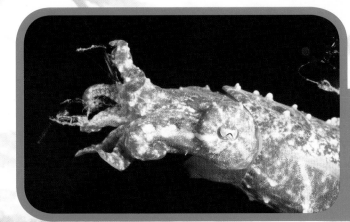

Mighty bite

A squid hunts small fish, shrimp, and crabs. Its strong beak can easily chomp through a crab's shell.

Crab hold!

Like other crabs, the red swimmer crab will eat almost anything it can grasp with its sharp pincers, including mussels, shrimp, snails, and plants. As their name suggests, these crabs are fast swimmers.

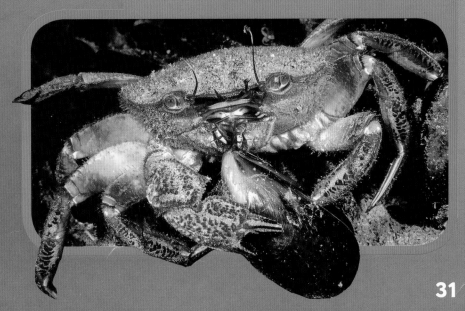

31

Doctor in the house

The powder blue surgeonfish is beautiful, but it can be fierce. It lives among coral reefs, where it feeds on algae. When a predator threatens it—look out! It's slashing time.

The **sharp teeth** are useful for tearing algae from rocks and coral.

Just like me

This fish doesn't go looking for trouble, but it will stand up for itself when threatened.

LOYAL FRIEND?

☐ YES ☒ NO

In the wild, the fish are sometimes seen in pairs or groups. But these fish can't be kept in an aquarium together or they will fight.

The **color** shows the fish's age. Young fish are mostly yellow; older fish are blue.

INFO BITES

Name: Powder Blue Surgeonfish

Type of animal: Fish

Home: Indian Ocean

Size: Up to 9 inches long. That's the size of a dinner plate.

The fish gets its name from the sharp, scalpel-like spines on its **tail.**

Indian Ocean

Powder Blue Surgeonfish Range

33

Egg-cellent parents

Many ocean animals lay eggs, instead of giving birth to babies. But that doesn't mean they aren't dedicated parents. These sea creatures go the extra mile looking after their eggs.

Mother love

A mama octopus gives it her all. She arranges her eggs—up to 56,000 of them—in a nest, and then spends six months guarding and protecting them. She never leaves, even to eat. Once her babies are born, her life is at its end.

Quite a mouthful

The male cardinalfish holds eggs in his mouth to protect them from predators. He can't eat until the babies are born.

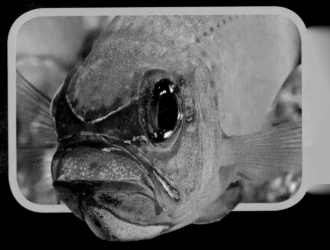

One of a kind

The male seahorse is the only male of any species to give birth to young. The female deposits eggs—as many as 2,000 at once—into a pouch on the male's stomach. In ten to 25 days, the babies are born.

Weight-lifters

Male marine whelks carry eggs around on their shells. Sometimes the dads are completely covered by their load of tiny whelks.

Whale of a tale

If you've been whale watching, you've probably seen a humpback whale. These whales stay near the shore. When it's time to dive, they breach the surface before plunging deep into the water. They communicate through songs filled with humming and wailing.

INFO BITES

Name: Humpback Whale

Type of animal: Mammal

Home: Near coastlines all over the world

Size: Up to 62 feet long and 80,000 pounds. A humpback whale is as big as a bulldozer.

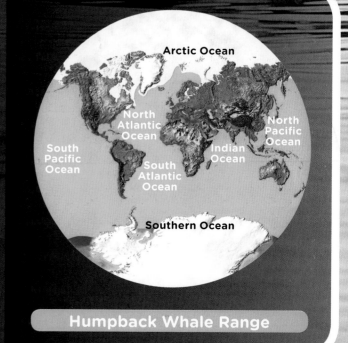

Humpback Whale Range

Pleats in the throat expand so the whale can take in more water while it's filter feeding.

The **flippers** are very long—up to one-third of the whale's length.

Just like me
Humpback whale mothers and babies are very close—they touch flippers as they swim, almost like holding hands.

SINGING FRIEND?

☒ ☐

YES   NO

Only males sing. No one knows why. It could be to attract females or to tell other whales where they are.

The stackup

beluga

Up to 18 feet long
and 3,500 pounds

gray whale

Up to 50 feet long
and 80,000 pounds

TALENT: HEAVY LIFTING

The gray whale lugs around barnacles,
whale lice, and other parasites. It takes
these freeloaders on a ride through
plankton-filled water.

sperm whale

Up to 60 feet long
and 100,000 pounds

fin whale

Up to 85 feet long
and 160,000 pounds

TALENT: MOVING FAST

The fin whale is the second-biggest
whale in the ocean, and it has a need
for speed. A fin whale can race
through the water at nearly 30 miles
per hour when it feels threatened.

blue whale

Up to 90 feet long
and 420,000 pounds

TALENT: HANGING OUT

Some pods of belugas migrate—very slowly, swimming no more than about nine miles per hour. Others just hang out in the same place all year round.

TALENT: DEEP DIVING

A sperm whale is the largest of any whale that has teeth. Its huge, box-shaped head can be up to 20 feet long. It can dive up to a mile deep.

TALENT: SPEAKING UP

Not only is it the biggest animal of all, but the blue whale is also the loudest animal on Earth. Its songs can be heard up to 1,000 miles in every direction.

39

School is cool

Do animals hang out together? Some do! A group of fish is called a school, but the fish aren't reading books. Ocean animals form groups for different reasons.

Come together

Little "bait" fish such as mackerel, herring, and sardines mass together for protection against predators. It's harder for a hunter to snatch a single fish from the group.

Birds of a feather

Seagulls form flocks that work together to find food, protect the group, and raise families. When they migrate, the gulls fly in formations that help them save energy while in the air.

Pod casts

Dolphins are highly social, and they explore the world in family groups called pods. Being part of a pod that works together makes it easier for the dolphins to hunt and to stay safe in the ocean.

Dance party!

Female great hammerheads will sometimes "dance" together. Large groups of these sharks have been seen nudging, bumping, and swirling around each other in their own special dance.

Just like me

Just like dolphins, people are social, too. We like to spend time with one another.

41

Whale, hello there!

These white whales swim in family groups, and they look like they're having fun. Belugas echolocate—that means they use sound to locate prey and to find their way in the ocean. They communicate through a language of clicks, hums, clangs, and whistles. They can even imitate other animals.

A curved **mouth** makes the beluga look like it's smiling. It's not—that's just how its mouth is shaped.

The **white color** develops as a baby beluga grows up. A beluga is born gray or brown.

LIFEGUARD-WORTHY?

[X] YES   [ ] NO

A beluga once rescued a struggling diver during a diving competition. The heroic whale pushed her to safety at the surface.

A **rounded forehead**, called a melon, helps the beluga echolocate.

A **smooth back** with no dorsal fin makes it easy for the beluga to slip under surface ice.

INFO BITES

Name: Beluga

Type of animal: Mammal

Home: Cold Arctic and sub-Arctic waters

Size: 13 to 20 feet long. A beluga is as long and heavy as a small ship.

Arctic Ocean

North Pacific Ocean

North Atlantic Ocean

North Pacific Ocean

Beluga Range

Just like me

Unlike other whales—but just like you—belugas have flexible necks that allow them to shake their heads back and forth and up and down.

Active with animals

Marine biologists and other scientists research marine life and make discoveries that help us better understand the mysteries of the oceans. Their work helps animals, too.

Curious study subjects

Manatees, also known as sea cows, are gentle, slow-moving mammals that live near coastlines. Marine biologists study them to monitor the health of the manatee population. Sometimes the animals are curious about the researchers, too!

Swim coach

When baby sea otters lose their moms, they need help learning how to swim. With a little coaching, eventually they can swim on their own.

Picture this

You don't have to get wet to study ocean life. Scientists use computers to track wildlife and analyze data while staying on land.

From the top down

Sharks are some of the most important predators in the sea. Experts want to know if their populations are growing or declining; if their habitat range has changed; if they are healthy or sickly. The answers to these questions will give us important information about sharks and the animals in the food web that sharks eat.

Caring for our oceans

More than 96 percent of Earth's water can be found in the oceans. They affect the air we breathe, our climate, and the weather. The oceans are an important source of food for animals and people, too.

In the web

When oil, sewage, and other pollutants end up in the ocean, marine creatures eat these harmful substances, spreading them throughout the food web.

Plastic peril

People have dumped huge amounts of plastic waste in the oceans, creating garbage patches. When animals eat the plastic, it can kill them.

Algae alert!

Fertilizers used by farmers to help grow crops drain into the oceans, causing fast-growing algae "blooms." Harmful algae blooms alter the balance of oxygen and nutrients in the oceans and endanger marine life.

Trash talk

Every year, volunteers participate in the International Coastal Cleanup and spend one day collecting garbage from shorelines around the world and counting what they find. Here are some of the things found during the 2015 cleanup effort.

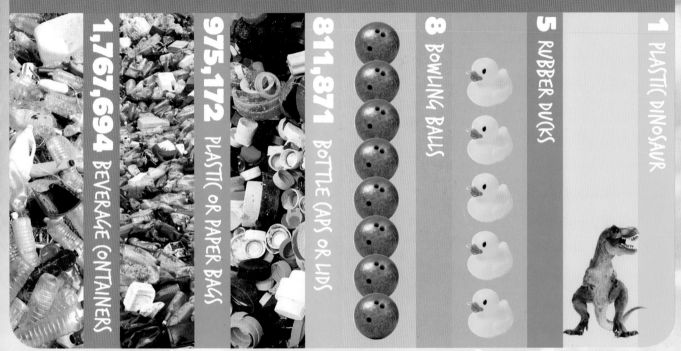

1,767,694 BEVERAGE CONTAINERS

975,172 PLASTIC OR PAPER BAGS

811,871 BOTTLE CAPS OR LIDS

8 BOWLING BALLS

5 RUBBER DUCKS

1 PLASTIC DINOSAUR

Success!

Helping to clean up our oceans and shorelines feels good! Here are some volunteers celebrating a haul of lost and discarded fishing nets removed from the ocean.

Reef life

A lively coral reef looks like an underwater garden. But reefs are made up of countless tiny animals called polyps. Thousands of plants and animals live in and around reefs, and all life on a reef is connected. Temperatures are warm here—never below 68° Fahrenheit.

Cleaner shrimp

The cleaner shrimp and moray eel help one another out. When a moray has that not-so-fresh feeling, it visits a "cleaning station," where a cleaner shrimp picks parasites off the eel. The shrimp, in turn, gets a good meal.

Vase sponge

A vase sponge provides a hiding place for crabs, shrimp, and other little sea critters like this grouper.

Tiger shark

The tiger shark patrols the waters around the reef in search of prey. This top hunter is important to reef life—it keeps the population of other reef animals from growing too large.

Crown-of-thorns sea star

The crown-of-thorns sea star is a predator, and the coral is its prey. Too many of these sea stars can kill a reef. Wrasses, triggerfish, and puffer fish eat them, helping to keep life on the reef in balance.

Christmas tree worm

Eek, worms! All kinds of worms live around the reef. A Christmas tree worm—named for its look-alike shape—digs its way into the coral and makes a home.

Puffed with pride

Puffer fish all bristle with defense mechanisms. When threatened by a predator, a puffer fish will gulp water to inflate itself into a hard-to-swallow ball. Some, like this porcupine fish, have pointed spines that pop out when they're inflated. If a predator does manage to eat the puffer, it will die from the fish's strong poison.

PLAY PAL-WORTHY?

☐ YES ☒ NO

Sadly, no. Those spines hurt! All of the fish's defense mechanisms are warnings to stay away.

INFO BITES

Name: Puffer Fish

Type of animal: Fish

Home: Tropical and temperate waters

Size: Puffer fish can be from 1 inch long to 4 feet long—the length of four hot dogs.

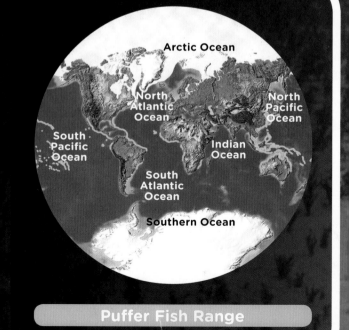

Arctic Ocean

North Atlantic Ocean

North Pacific Ocean

South Pacific Ocean

Indian Ocean

South Atlantic Ocean

Southern Ocean

Puffer Fish Range

Tiny fins make this puffer fish a slow swimmer.

Spines expand when this puffer fish is inflated.

The **skin** is stretchy so the fish can expand and then return to its normal size.

Just like me

A puffer fish's stomach gets bigger when it swallows water. Your belly expands when you eat and drink a lot, too.

Jellies galore

Pretty

Jellyfish come in all shapes and sizes. Many can sting in self-defense, and some contain venom that can even be fatal to humans. They are colorful creatures.

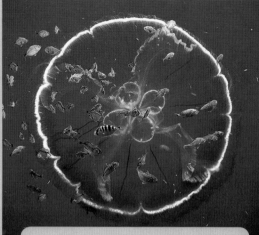

Moon jelly

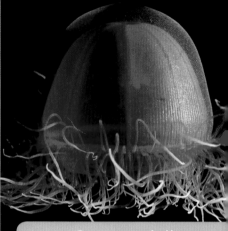

Crossota jelly

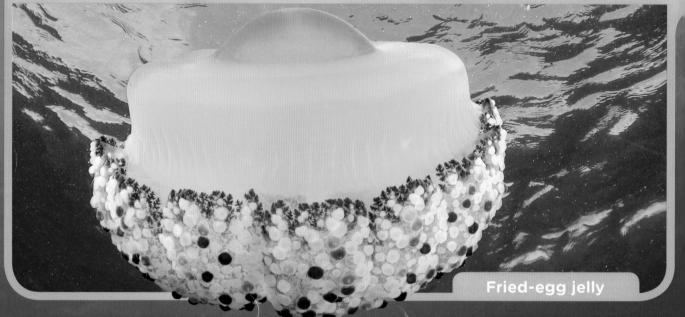

Fried-egg jelly

Anemone

Rabbitfish

Sea star

Porpita jelly

Red comb jelly

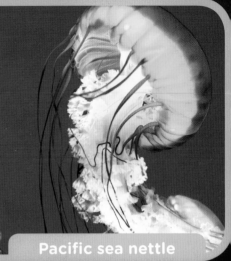

Pacific sea nettle

Green sea turtle

Boxfish

Crown butterflyfish

Pretty tasty

It's a jelly-eat-jelly world. Jellies eat plankton, small fish, crustaceans, and even other jellies. Lots of marine animals find jellies good enough to eat, too.

Cool crib

Blacktip reef sharks spend the first year of their lives in shark nurseries, learning the skills they will need as adults.

Angling for dinner

A female anglerfish tempts prey with a glowing spine that sticks out of her head. It looks like a worm. It brings prey close enough for the anglerfish to pounce. Only the females fish.

INFO BITES

Name: Anglerfish

Type of animal: Fish

Home: Far below the surface of the Atlantic and the Arctic oceans

Size: Most anglerfish are about a foot long, but some grow to 3 feet long. A guitar is 3 feet long.

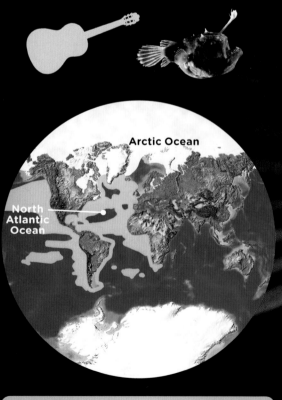

Arctic Ocean

North Atlantic Ocean

Anglerfish Range

The **skin** contains chemicals that produce light.

The **"fishing rod" spine** has a glow-in-the-dark lure. Bacteria in the lure make it glow.

BOTTOM-DWELLING BUD?

☐ YES ☒ NO

An anglerfish may look alluring, but it's just trying to find some food to eat.

Eyesight is very poor, but the anglerfish doesn't need to see well where it lives.

Translucent teeth are hard to see in the dark, deep ocean.

Unusual lookers

Funny faces

Ocean animals have lots of different faces and shapes. Some have super big eyes and unusual body parts. Others look just plain funny to us.

Peacock mantis shrimp

Humphead wrasse

Longhorn cowfish

Venus flytrap anemone

Fringeback nudibranch

Squat lobster

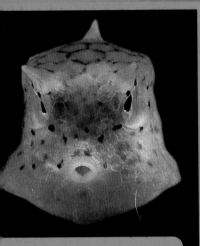

Juvenile boxfish

Spotted moray eel

Bobtail squid

Great hammerhead shark

Dumbo octopus

Gumboot chiton

Weird and cool

There are thousands of varieties of fish and ocean creatures. Some look cool, some look weird, and some look just a little scary.

All for one

The Portuguese man-of-war looks like a jelly, but it isn't one. It's a siphonophore—an animal made up of a colony of organisms working together. As the colony drifts on the surface of the water, its long tentacles dangle down. The stinging tentacles are covered in strong venom.

INFO BITES

Name: Portuguese Man-of-War

Type of animal: Invertebrate

Home: Usually tropical and subtropical waters, but starting to inhabit cooler water

Size: Tentacles can dangle 30 to 165 feet into the ocean. It can be as long as a lighthouse is tall.

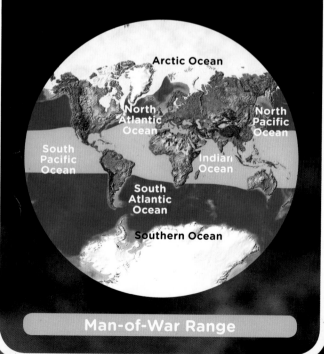

Arctic Ocean

North Atlantic Ocean

North Pacific Ocean

South Pacific Ocean

Indian Ocean

South Atlantic Ocean

Southern Ocean

Man-of-War Range

FUN AT THE BEACH?

☐ YES ☒ NO

No way! A man-of-war's sting is extremely painful and can even be deadly to people.

The **sail** gives the animal its name. People thought it looked like a Portuguese warship with the wind in its sails.

A **gas-filled sac** forms the top of the man-of-war. This sac keeps the colony floating near the surface.

Just like me
A man-of-war gets around the ocean by floating in the direction the wind and ocean currents take it. Can you float and swim?

Colors range from blue to pink to purple.

Venomous tentacles are used to trap and paralyze prey.

Exploring the oceans

Scientists spend long periods of time on research ships so they can study the ocean's different areas, or ecosystems. What's it like to live and work on the ocean? Follow this journey of exploration and see.

Lights, camera, action!

Remotely operated cameras record what's going on in the ocean. They are dropped over the side of the ship on a platform called a sled.

Mission control

Researchers on board the ship monitor underwater cameras remotely. They can observe the deep-sea realm and transmit data to scientists elsewhere.

Scaredy-fish

Not ready for its close-up, this eelpout scurries to burrow under the sand.

Okeanos Explorer is used by the National Oceanic and Atmospheric Administration (NOAA) for ocean research.

Look who's here!

The underwater camera spotted this squat lobster on black coral. Deep-water coral doesn't need light to grow, so it can live in dark waters.

Undersea mountains

Computer imaging helps marine scientists learn about canyons and mountains on the ocean floor. This technology makes it possible to create accurate maps.

Eight is great

A common octopus seems like it would be an easy snack for a hungry hunter. However, amazing adaptations help it evade predators. It can use camouflage, squirt ink, squeeze into a tiny space, or just swim away fast to stay alive. It can even let go of a tentacle to escape—it can regrow it later.

Eight arms give the octopus its name—it's from a Greek word meaning "eight-footed."

Special receptors on the octopus's skin help it perceive light and color.

Just like me

Octopuses are smart! They have been observed in captivity opening jar lids to get to tasty shrimp inside.

The **suckers** are superstrong. One large sucker can hold 35 pounds. Each arm has about 240 suckers.

INFO BITES

Name: Common Octopus

Type of animal: Invertebrate

Home: Tropical and temperate waters

Size: Up to 3 feet long and 22 pounds. That's the weight of two average-sized house cats.

Arctic Ocean

North Atlantic Ocean

North Pacific Ocean

South Pacific Ocean

Indian Ocean

South Atlantic Ocean

Southern Ocean

Common Octopus Range

HUG-WORTHY?

☐ YES   ☒ NO

You don't want to hug an octopus. Its beaklike jaws can deliver a nasty bite, and its saliva is full of venom.

Clever camouflage

Blending

Some ocean animals blend in with their habitat, matching colors and patterns. This helps them escape notice from predators looking for something good to eat.

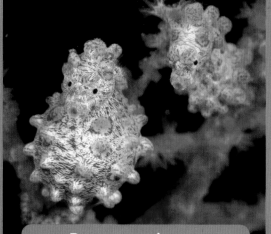

Pygmy seahorse

Freckled hawkfish

Porcelain crab

Blenny

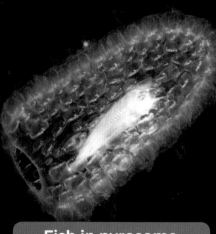

Fish in pyrosome

Longfin snake eel

assled scorpion fish

Ghost pipefish

Painted frogfish

Jeweled anemone crab

Coconut octopus

Goby fish

Hiding

To hide from predators, some ocean animals tuck into coral crevices, some burrow below the sand, while others find discarded shells that they turn into hideouts.

Don't be shellfish

Hermit crabs live in the discarded shells of other creatures. When a crab finds a promising new shell that is too big, it will hang around until other crabs show up. More crabs gather to wait for shells that fit perfectly, forming a line in size order. Then each one climbs out of its shell and moves into the next size up!

A **hard exoskeleton** that was originally from another animal protects the crab's soft body.

The crab has **two sets of antennae**. Feelers touch what is around the crab, and antennules make it possible for the crab to taste and smell.

GOOD PET PAL?

[X] YES   [X] NO

Yes and no. Hermit crabs are sold as pets, but wild crabs live much longer than pet crabs do.

Just like me

Hermit crabs need bigger and bigger shells as they grow... just like you need bigger and bigger clothes.

The **hairs** on the exoskeleton are called setae, and they help the crab feel what is around it.

The **second and third leg pairs** are used for walking. The hermit crab has ten legs.

INFO BITES

Name: Hermit Crab

Type of animal: Crustacean

Home: Wherever there are coastlines

Size: As small as ¼ inch long and up to 8 inches long. The longest is about the size of a fork.

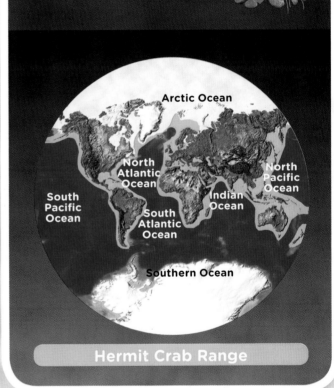

Arctic Ocean

North Atlantic Ocean

North Pacific Ocean

South Pacific Ocean

Indian Ocean

South Atlantic Ocean

Southern Ocean

Hermit Crab Range

Coral corral

A coral reef is made up of countless tiny animals called polyps. Sea creatures and plants live in and around the reef, forming an amazing ecosystem.

Extreme animals

Life in the ocean is varied, but these underwater creatures are exceptional even by ocean standards.

SMALLEST FRY

The dwarf goby fish holds the record for littlest fish. Head to tail, a full-grown fish is only ¼ inch long. It's little, but lovely, with strikingly colorful eyes and a transparent body.

SHORT STUFF

This tiny pygmy shark lives up to its name. With females topping out at about 11 inches, and males even smaller than that, it's one of the smallest

SEA SMARTS

An octopus can observe, learn, and behave in complex ways. It has the largest brain of any invertebrate.

OPEN ARMS

The feather sea star has more arms than most sea stars—the better to catch food going by. It uses its ten arms, each with many branches, to filter food and move around.

THAT'S HAIRY!

Sea otters have more hairs per square inch than any other animal— about 1 million. Why so many? Dense hair keeps them warm in cold water.

ROYAL HUE

Even in the colorful ocean, this bright purple sea star is a real standout.

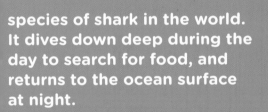

species of shark in the world. It dives down deep during the day to search for food, and returns to the ocean surface at night.

Ocean activities

TURTLE RALLY

Baby sea turtles hatch from eggs on the beach, then race to the ocean as fast as their little flippers will take them. How fast can you race from beach to ocean?.

What you'll need:
• 2 pieces of string or rope, each about 8 feet long
• 4 players
• 1 person to call "Go" and determine the winner

1. In an open space outside or indoors, stretch out a length of rope—this will be the "beach."

2. Take twenty steps forward and stretch out the second piece of rope—this will be the "water."

3. Get down on your bellies on the "beach." When the timer calls "Go," race to the "water." Use your arms and legs the way turtles use their flippers.

The first "baby turtle" to reach the water wins!

UNDERWATER STATUES

Fish move in different ways. Sailfish speed along and jump out of the water. Eels wriggle along in a wavy way. Crabs crawl sideways. An octopus twists and turns. But what would they look like if they stopped in mid-movement?

What you'll need:
• Music player
• 2 or more players
• 1 person to start and stop the music

1. Make a list of different fish in this book and how they move. You can check back on Liquid Locomotion to get started.

2. Get your friends together. Each person can choose an ocean animal to be.

3. When the timer starts the music, begin moving like the ocean animal you chose. When the music stops, freeze in place.

Take turns and try out all the ocean animals on your list. There aren't any winners or losers—just lots of fun and giggles!

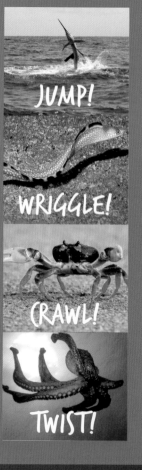

JUMP!

WRIGGLE!

CRAWL!

TWIST!

DIVE IN!

What you'll need:
• Drawing paper
• Crayons or markers

Imagine you're a scuba diver exploring a coral reef. What animals do you see? Is there a butterflyfish? A clownfish tucked into its favorite sea anemone? Is there a sea turtle swimming by? Draw a picture of your underwater adventure and share it with your friends and family.

Resources

FIND OUT MORE

Continue your ocean adventure and explore more amazing animals by reading more books, checking out interesting websites, and visiting aquariums, museums, and zoos.

PLACES TO VISIT

UNITED STATES

**Monterey Bay Aquarium
Monterey, CA
montereybayaquarium.org**
Located at the edge of Monterey Bay, this is a great place to spot marine life in the wild—from sea otters to whales. Features include the Open Sea exhibit, where tuna, sharks, and schools of sardines swim past. The Thriving Ocean Wildlife program focuses on ocean conservation.

**Georgia Aquarium
Atlanta, GA
georgiaaquarium.org**
This is the only aquarium in North America big enough to house whale sharks, the world's largest fish, along with belugas, penguins, rays, and many other ocean animals. The aquarium is also committed to rescue and rehabilitation programs for sea lions, sea turtles, and sea otters.

**Waikiki Aquarium
Honolulu, HI
waikikiaquarium.org**
Local marine life is featured in the Hawaiian Marine Communities exhibit. The Amazing Adaptations Gallery showcases sea horses, sea dragons, and pipefish from around the world.

**Shedd Aquarium
Chicago, IL
sheddaquarium.org**
Housing one of the world's largest displays of marine life, Shedd Aquarium brings visitors within inches of a huge variety of marine animals. Tour a reef at the Caribbean Reef exhibit. Get a diver's view of sharks, stingrays, and live coral in the Wild Reef exhibit. Spot belugas, Pacific white-sided dolphins, sea lions, and sea otters at the Abbott Oceanarium.

**Newport Aquarium
Newport, KY
newportaquarium.com**
Get immersed in the ocean by walking through the tunnels of the Surrounded by Sharks exhibit. Shark Bridge, a 75-foot-long rope bridge, gives a topside view of sharks, rays, and fish in an open-air tank display.

**Audubon Aquarium of the Americas
New Orleans, LA
auduboninstitute.org/aquarium**
The 40,000-gallon Gulf of Mexico exhibit is packed with sharks, stingrays, schools of fish, and sea turtles, including an endangered green sea turtle. Experience harsh ocean weather in the hurricane simulator.

**National Aquarium
Baltimore, MD
aqua.org**
Dolphin Discovery, the aquarium's largest exhibit, is home to a pod of eight bottlenose dolphins. In the Blacktip Reef exhibit, sharks swim with the divers who feed them. At the Living Seashore exhibit, visitors can touch a variety of sea creatures, from moon snails to jellies.

**New England Aquarium
Boston, MA
neaq.org**
The four-story Ocean Tank contains a coral reef with hundreds of Caribbean reef animals, including sea turtles, stingrays, eels, and fish. A colony of more than 80 penguins, including rockhoppers and little blue penguins, lives at the aquarium.

**New York Aquarium
Brooklyn, NY
nyaquarium.com**
See walruses and penguins in the Sea Cliffs exhibit and sea lions at the Aquatheater. Penguin, sea otter, and walrus feedings are daily attractions. The aquarium features more than 8,000 animals.

**Oregon Coast Aquarium
Newport, OR
aquarium.org**
The Octopus Encounter includes a behind-the-scenes tour and educational information about the giant Pacific octopus. Other exhibits feature sea lions, sea otters, reef fish, marine birds, and much more.

**Dallas World Aquarium
Dallas, TX
dwazoo.com**
The 20,000-gallon walk-through tunnel exhibit is home to hundreds of coral reef animals, including anemones, seahorses, and a vast array of fish.

CANADA

**Shaw Ocean Discovery Centre
Sidney, BC
oceandiscovery.ca**
This science museum has more than 3,500 animals, from a giant Pacific octopus to sculpins, sea stars to anemones, and jellies galore. With hands-on workshops, a touch pool, and tours and activities, this aquarium of the Salish Sea is for kids of all ages.

**Vancouver Aquarium
Vancouver, BC
vanaqua.org**
This aquarium is home to more than 50,000 species. Visitors can explore the animals in different habitats, from the Tropic Zone to Penguin Point. There are kid-friendly tours giving close-up looks at sea lions, dolphins, and sea otters.

**Ripley's Aquarium of Canada
Toronto, ON
ripleyaquariums.com/canada/**
The country's largest aquarium is home to more than 13,000 aquatic animals of 450 different species, held in nearly 1.6 million gallons of water. Visitors have the opportunity to touch crabs and stingrays, go behind the scenes, and "sleep with sharks" during an overnight stay beneath a shark tank.

BOOKS

ANIMALS: A VISUAL ENCYCLOPEDIA
Meet more than 2,500 amazing animals in this comprehensive, family-fun, global reference guide from Animal Planet—your source for all things animal. Explore the many ways animals are just like us. The book includes more than 1,000 stunning photos!

POLAR ANIMALS
A companion to OCEAN ANIMALS, this Animal Bites book takes the reader from the tippy-top of the planet to the very bottom. Learn about the animals that call the North and South Poles home, and see how and where they live.

WEBSITES

You can visit all of the zoos online to learn more. Here are some additional websites to check out.

apl.tv
Check out the Animal Planet L!VE cams to see a revolving feature of live-action animal videos, from feeding time with penguins to close-ups of coral reef fish and sea otters.

discoverykids.com
Check out sharks, penguins, and many other animals, play games, and watch videos at this entertaining animal site for kids.

oceanservice.noaa.gov/kids
Start here to find many informative and fun websites from the National Oceanic and Atmospheric Association. Learn about marine life and habitats, explore the deep sea, and find fun activities and photos galore.

climatekids.nasa.gov
Learn about the oceans, animals, and Earth's climate; play games; watch videos; and find crafts and activities on this informative and fun kid-friendly website from the National Aeronautics and Space Administration.

Glossary

abyss An area of the ocean below the midnight zone. The abyss can be 20,000 feet deep.

algae Tiny plants found in oceans, lakes, and other bodies of water.

algae bloom A rapid overgrowth of algae.

anemone A colorful, stinging sea creature that looks like a flower.

Antarctic Relating to the South Pole.

Arctic Relating to the North Pole.

▼ baleen Stiff, fingernail-like material in the mouths of some whales. Baleen is used to separate krill from ocean water.

*A humpback whale filters fish to eat with its **baleen**.*

billfish A fish with long, slender jaws. Sailfish, swordfish, and marlins are billfish.

breach To leap out of the water. Whales and dolphins breach.

camouflage A way of hiding by blending in with the surroundings.

cephalopod A type of ocean mollusk that has tentacles on its head. Octopuses are cephalopods.

cold-blooded Having a body temperature not regulated by the body and close to that of the environment. Fish are cold-blooded.

conservation The protection of animals, plants, and natural resources.

countershading A pattern of coloration in which a sea animal is light colored on the bottom and dark on the top. This coloration makes it hard for a predator to see the animal.

crustacean A type of animal that has several pairs of legs and a hard outer shell. Crabs and lobsters are crustaceans.

echolocation A way of using sound waves to find prey and other objects. Dolphins use echolocation.

equator An imaginary line around the middle of the earth. It's hot by the equator.

▼ exoskeleton The outer supportive or protective covering of an animal.

*An **exoskeleton** protects the Sally Lightfoot crab.*

food web The complex network of food chains in a habitat.

habitat The place where an animal usually lives, or an area where different animals live together.

hydrothermal vent A spout on the ocean floor where hot water shoots out from volcanic cracks.

▼ invertebrate An animal without a spine.

*A European cuttlefish is an **invertebrate**.*

jellyfish A sea creature with a soft body and stinging tentacles.

krill A type of zooplankton. Krill are like tiny shrimp.

mammal An animal that produces milk to feed its young, has hair on its body, and has a backbone. Humans and whales are mammals.

marine biologist A scientist who studies different aspects of ocean life.

midnight zone An area at the bottom of the ocean. It is always dark there.

migration The movement of animals from one place to another place according to the season.

mollusk A type of animal that has a soft body and lives in a shell. Clams and snails are mollusks.

nematocyst A stinger on the tentacle of a jelly.

oceanography The study of the oceans.

parasite An animal that lives on or in another animal, taking food and protection from it.

▼ pectoral fin The front fin of fish and other marine animals.

*A humpback whale can wave its **pectoral fin** while its body is underwater.*

plankton Very small plant and animal life in oceans, lakes, and other water. Phytoplankton are tiny plants. Zooplankton are tiny animals.

pod A group of whales or dolphins.

polyp A tiny sea animal with a tube-shaped body. Coral is made up of many polyps.

predator An animal that hunts and eats other animals.

prey An animal that is eaten by other animals.

school A group of fish.

▼ siphonophore A type of floating organism. Most siphonophores are long, thin, and jellylike.

*A **siphonophore** dwells in deep waters.*

sunlight zone The area at the top of the ocean that gets the most sunlight.

swim bladder An organ inside a fish that holds air. It helps the fish float.

tentacle A long arm used for grabbing and movement. Octopuses have tentacles.

twilight zone An area in the middle of the ocean. It is deeper than the sunlight zone but not as deep as the midnight zone.

undulate To move in a wavy motion, like an eel.

venom Toxin produced by an animal and passed to a victim, usually through a bite or a sting.

▼ vertebrate An animal with a spine.

*You are a **vertebrate**, and your spine helps you stand.*

warm-blooded Having a relatively high, constant body temperature that is independent of the environment. Birds and mammals are warm-blooded animals.

Index

Photo credits

Produced by
Scout Books & Media Inc
President and Project Director
Susan Knopf
Writer Laaren Brown
Project Manager and Editor
Margaret Parrish
Assistant Editor and Photo Researcher Brittany Gialanella
Photo and Editorial Researcher
Chelsea Burris
Copyeditor Stephanie Engel
Proofreader Michael Centore
Editorial Intern Faith Krech
Indexer Sarah Schott

Designer Dirk Kaufman
Prepress by Andrij Borys Associates, LLC

Advisor Andy Dehart
VP of Animal Husbandry, Patricia and Philip Frost Museum of Science

Special thanks to the Time Inc. Books team: Margot Schupf, Steve Koepp, Beth Sutinis, Deirdre Langeland, Georgia Morrissey, Megan Pearlman, and Stephanie Braga.

Special thanks to the Discovery and Animal Planet Creative and Licensing Teams: Tracy Connor, Elizabeta Ealy, Robert Harick, Doris Miller, Sue Perez-Jackson, and Janet Tsuei.

© 2015 Discovery Communications, LLC. ANIMAL PLANET™ and the logos are trademarks of Discovery Communications, LLC, used under license. All rights reserved.

LIBERTY STREET

Published by Liberty Street, an imprint of Time Inc. Books
225 Liberty Street
New York, NY 10281

LIBERTY STREET is a trademark of Time Inc.

All rights reserved. No part of this book may be reproduced in any form or by any electronic or mechanical means, including information storage and retrieval systems, without permission in writing from the publisher, except by a reviewer, who may quote brief passages in a review.

ISBN 10: 1-61893-162-8
ISBN 13: 978-1-61893-162-7

First edition, 2015

Printed and bound in China

1 TLF 15

Time Inc. Books may be purchased for business or promotional use. For information on bulk purchases, please contact Ilene Schreider in the Special Sales Department at (212) 522-3985.

To order Time Inc. Books Collector's Editions, please call (800) 327-6388, Monday through Friday, 7 a.m.-9 p.m., Central Time.

We welcome your comments and suggestions about Time Inc. Books. Please write to us at:
Time Inc. Books
Attention: Book Editors
P.O. Box 62310
Tampa, FL 33662-2310

timeincbooks.com